Romance of Flowers

Romance of Flowers

Pat Poce

Sterling Publishing Co., Inc.
New York

A Sterling/Chapelle Book

Chapelle Ltd.

Owner: Jo Packham

Editor: Leslie Ridenour

Writer: Kimberly Maw

Staff: Areta Bingham, Kass Burchett, Marilyn Goff, Holly Hollingsworth, Susan Jorgensen, Barbara Milburn, Linda Orton, Karmen Quinney, Cindy Stoeckl, Gina Swapp, Kim Taylor, Sara Toliver, Kristi Torsak

Photography: Kevin Dilley for Hazen Photography, Scot Zimmerman

Special Thanks
Thanks to Clyde and Pat Buehler, Shannon McBride, Ted and Sheri Morgan, Scott and Carol Nelson, Jo Packham, Gene and CarolLynne Smith, and Chuck and Julie Smith for allowing us to photograph in the beautiful settings of their homes.

Author's Acknowledgments
A very special thanks to my family, staff, and friends of The Posy Place. Without their time and efforts, I would not have been able to undertake a project of this magnitude.

Library of Congress Cataloging-in-Publication Data Available

Poce, Patrick.
  The romance of flowers / Patrick Poce.
    p.cm.
  "A Sterling/Chapelle book."
  ISBN 0-8069-6647-5
  1.Flower arrangement. I. Title.

SB449.P587 2001
745.92'2--dc21

00-053779

A Sterling/Chapelle Book

Published by Sterling Publishing Company, Inc.
387 Park Avenue South, New York, NY 10016
© 2001 by Pat Poce
Distributed in Canada by Sterling Publishing
⅟ Canadian Manda Group, One Atlantic Avenue, Suite 105
Toronto, Ontario, Canada M6K 3E7
Distributed in Great Britain and Europe by Cassell PLC
Wellington House, 125 Strand, London WC2R 0BB, England
Distributed in Australia by Capricorn Link (Australia) Pty Ltd.
P.O. Box 6651, Baulkham Hills, Business Centre, NSW 2153, Australia
Printed in China
All Rights Reserved

Sterling ISBN 0-8069-6647-5

If you have any questions or comments, please contact:

Chapelle Ltd., Inc.
P.O. Box 9252
Ogden, UT 84409
Phone: (801) 621-2777
FAX: (801) 621-2788
e-mail:
Chapelle@chapelleltd.com
website: www.chapelleltd.com

For more information on designs by Pat Poce, please contact:

The Posy Place
2757 Washington Blvd.
Ogden, UT 84401
(801) 621-4010

About the Author

Pat Poce, AIFD has been designing with flowers for more than 30 years. Born and raised in Ogden, Utah, he attended private school and later studied art at Weber State University in Ogden. Pat worked in several floral stores before he decided to open his own floral design business, The Posy Place, in 1977.

He attributes his fascination with flowers to his childhood—being allowed to help his parents grow plants and flowers which they entered in the Utah State Fair. His father, Bill Poce, was a multiple state fair winner with Dahlia, Begonia, and Gladiolus.

Pat has been involved in the floral industry at a local, regional, and national level. He has served on several local association committees and has served as chairman of the Teleflora, Northwest Florists' Association, Utah Allied Florists, and FTD Association conventions.

He participated as a member of different design teams that provided spectacular floral arrangements for several national events including a White House Reception hosted by President and Mrs. Reagan, the Statue of Liberty Restoration Celebration, the Inauguration of President Clinton in 1993, and for the 1996 Summer Olympics in Atlanta. He has also designed for various panels in Canada, South America, and locations across the United States.

Pat is a member of the Ogden/Weber Chamber of Commerce, the Society of American Florists, the American Institute of Floral Design, and is an FTD Certified Master Designer. He has been involved with community events and volunteered for organizations such as the Utah Opera Guild, Northern Utah Hospice, Planned Parenthood of Utah, Utah AIDS Foundation, Ogden Nature Center, and Eccles Art Center in Ogden. He often donates his time and product to local high schools and enjoys working with and encouraging young florists who are getting started in the industry.

About This Book

When I think of romance, I think of any beautiful expression of love, given with an open heart. Romance is a way of living, a way of filling and surrounding your life and the lives of the people you love with objects and images that nourish the senses.

Flowers do just that—through touch, sight, and smell. They can calm and comfort, excite and awaken, and communicate volumes without ever saying a word.

The purpose of this book is to awaken your imagination to all the wonderful ways and reasons to arrange and give flowers. Herein, I have gathered stories, myths, journal notes, poems, and thoughts written by kindred spirits from varied places and times to help illustrate romantic, loving ways to express yourself through flowers.

Flowers need not be extravagant, complex, or expensive to be breathtaking and thoughtful. They can range from the traditional dozen red roses at Valentines' Day to a single gardenia floating in a small, crystal bowl. Don't feel you can only give flowers on big, special occasions. You can give flowers to anyone, at any time, for any reason or no reason at all. Not only to your sweetheart, but to a dear aunt, neighbor, father, close friend, or coworker. They will make any recipient feel loved and special. Almost everyone can recall the last time they received flowers!

Also, you do not need to leave the flower arranging to the professional florist and the delivery boy. Many of the arrangements here are very simple to do. Today, many supermarket and street vendors sell a wide variety of flowers, waiting to be arranged, at very reasonable prices. The directions in this book will give you the basics you'll need to create beautiful designs. Feel free to exchange these flowers for others that are more common in your area, or change the colors to perfectly suit your message. Choose your own type of containers as well from the wide variety of pots, bowls, baskets, and mugs that are available. How much more memorable it will be to give your loved ones flowers that you arranged yourself, especially for them.

If, however, you would like to have a design done by a professional, do not hesitate to take this book in when you visit your florist. This will make communicating with him so much easier and will help him create just the design you want.

Let the designs and thoughts that follow be a springboard for your own creations. Come wander among these blossoms with me, and see how easy it is to fill your life and the lives of those you love with the Romance of Flowers.

Getting Started

The following pages provide instructions for how to prepare flowers to put into arrangements. Some information is specific to a particular flower and some will apply generally.

Tools & Supplies

Supplies generally needed for floral design include: ribbon shears; clippers; 18-, 21-, and 24-gauge floral wire in green or light green; floral clay adhesive; water tubes; green, light green, and brown floral tape; knife; wire cutters; Gerbera Daisy stem sleeves; 4" and 6" wooden picks; and ½"-wide waterproof tape (not shown).

Basic Rules for Arranging Flowers

Always trim stems at an angle, giving a larger surface area to absorb water. Stand flowers in cool to lukewarm water to hasten absorption. Remove all leaves below water level to prevent bacterial growth, which shortens the life of the flowers.

Keep flowers out of direct heat and cold and out of sunlight to prolong the life of the arrangement. To revive an arrangement, recut the ends of the flowers, change the water, and add commercial flower food or conditioner.

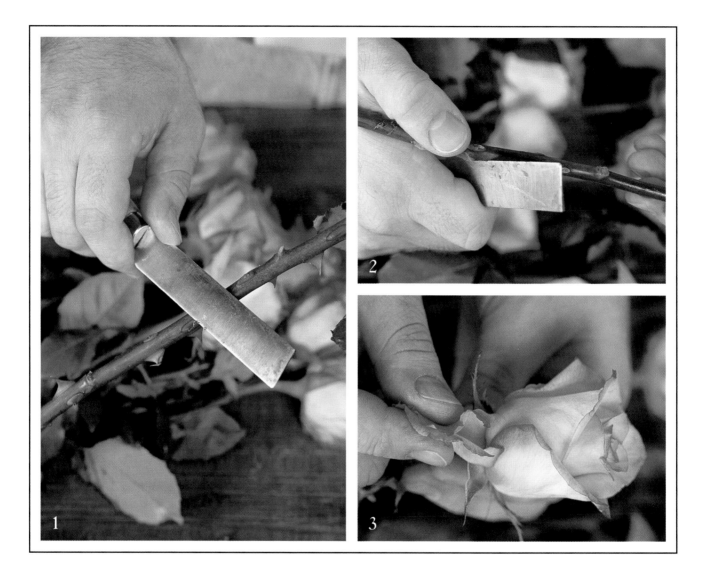

For best results when using roses, they should be cleaned and cared for properly. Using a sharp knife and taking care not to damage the bark of the rose stem, remove all thorns and foliage that will be below the water level. Cut approximately 1" from the end of the stem and place the stem in clean lukewarm water. Add floral food or preservative to the water if desired.

Remove the "guard" or outer few petals of the rose which may be dark or bruised by gently pulling the petal from the top of the rose and debauching it from the bottom.

Visualize what the finished arrangement will look like before you start so that you have a plan to follow.

Begin the arrangement by building the framework of the design with flowers or foliage. Establish the height and then the width. As a general rule, the height of your arrangement should be one-and-a-half to two times the height of your container. For example, in the arrangement on page 26 the glass cylinder is 24" and the gladiolus were cut 36" long. The width of the arrangement is usually about the same as the height. Build your arrangement from the outside, working inward. Choose your focal point and build around it. Cut some flowers short to create depth. Add flowers and foliage for balance and then fill in the design with more flowers and foliage.

Large areas of foliage can be used to visually pull the center of the arrangement together. They can also form a background for special blooms or fruit.

Do not place choice, central flowers or any delicate blooms until you are near the end of your arrangement as they may become damaged as you try to work around them. You may put them in to envision what the end result will look like, but then remove them before you continue with the arrangement.

Try to distribute flowers of one type throughout the arrangement, unless it is a small flower that can be clumped together rather than spread about. Generally, stems which are placed side by side should not be of the same length.

Arrange some flowers or foliage softly over the edge of the container at the sides and front to break any straight line that may occur at the base of the arrangement. Curved or lightweight pieces are ideal here. Breaking the line also helps the container and its contents appear as one unit rather than separate parts.

Step back from the arrangement from time to time for an overall view. Look at it from the side also if it will be seen from that angle. If it is for a dining table, check that the height is correct and that it will not interfere with the seated guest's vision.

Containers

Containers should accent or support the floral design not compete with it. Containers can include vases, pots, baskets, ceramic canisters, or even a wooden salad set.

Make certain that the flower size and height are correct for the scale of your container and vice versa. Containers should be sturdy and heavy enough to support the weight of the flowers. Be aware that water will also add to the weight of the container.

Make certain your container does not leak and that its bottom is dry. Place the container so it is level and secure and with any features, such as handles, in their correct position.

If possible, put your container in the place where it is going to stand—especially if the container is large and/or heavy. Some containers are so large that they would not be moveable when full of water. Make certain to have a watering can nearby if you are going to have to carry water to the container. The scale of your arrangement is also more likely to be correct if it can be done in the place it will stand. If this is not possible, try to arrange the design on a similar level.

Flowers

When choosing flowers, select both mature blooms and immature buds. Intersperse these in your arrangement so that blooms continue to open, extending the life of the bouquet.

Select flowers and foliage that are representative of the theme or mood you are trying to create. For example, use tropical foliage with tropical flowers for a tropical theme. Be very careful when mixing exotics with the more common types of flowers.

Some flowers, such as Oncidium orchids, have a certain fluidity to them. They add movement to the design of the arrangement. When an arrangement is given, these communicate motion—as if the arrangement is moving toward the receiver.

Choose flowers with stems as long as possible so you can choose where to place them in the arrangement. They can be cut down, if necessary, once you choose where to place them.

Think twice before throwing away broken or leftover flower heads. These can create quite an artistic piece when placed in a low container.

Foliage
Choose foliages to supplement and complement flowers.

Foliage, such as ruscus, helps to tighten a design so flowers will stay in place when the arrangement is moved.

Foliage is often used to create negative space—forming the shape of the design but not drawing attention.

Some foliage, such as eucalyptus, communicates the same sort of motion as mentioned with flowers. Whenever possible, try to use these types of foliage in an arrangement that will be given.

The natural appearance of some types of foliage, such as this Ti leaf, can be altered for added dimension in your arrangements. Roll the Ti leaf underneath itself and secure the tip to the stem with green floral tape. For added luster, use spray-on leaf shine.

Ornaments & Props

Many of the arrangements in this book contain design elements that are not classified as flowers or foliage. To use ornaments that most often do not have a suitable stem, such as gourds, squash, pumpkins, bread, peppers, and seed balls insert a wooden pick into the base of each ornament.

Arrangements are often built up around props and ordinary objects are modified slightly for use as flower containers. Props can include glass flowers, metal birdhouses, plush toys, kitchen implements, or a bread bowl like this one.

To make the Bread Bowl on page 79, slice off the top of the bread bowl. Hollow out the bread and place a small container, such as a spray can lid, filled with floral foam into the bread. Start at the base of the foam with a fern or green material, such as seeded eucalyptus. Next, add Hypericum, at the top of the foam. Finish with a few flowers at the center.

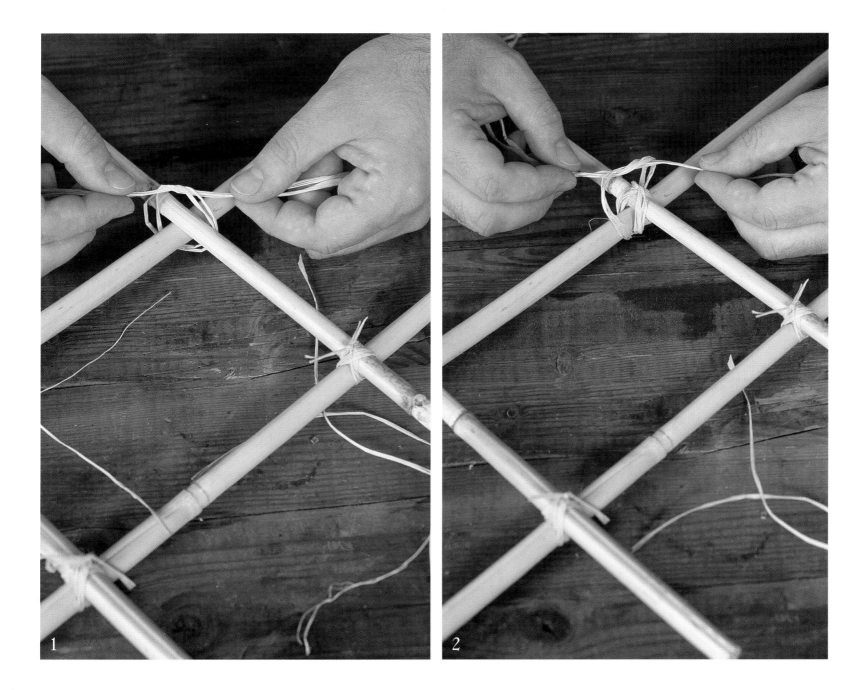

This bamboo trellis is constructed to prop and arrangement by first measuring the long pieces and cutting them carefully with a sharp knife. Next, the cross pieces are measured and cut. Bind the shorter cross pieces to the long bamboo with 18" lengths of raffia. Knot the raffia on the top, cross and tie diagonally, and knot again on the top. Trim the raffia to desired length.

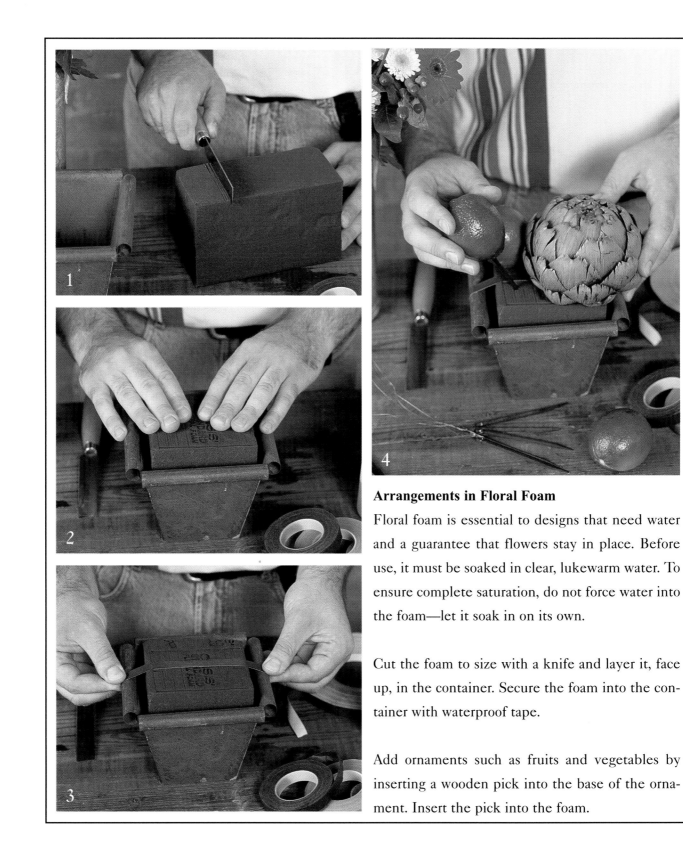

Arrangements in Floral Foam

Floral foam is essential to designs that need water and a guarantee that flowers stay in place. Before use, it must be soaked in clear, lukewarm water. To ensure complete saturation, do not force water into the foam—let it soak in on its own.

Cut the foam to size with a knife and layer it, face up, in the container. Secure the foam into the container with waterproof tape.

Add ornaments such as fruits and vegetables by inserting a wooden pick into the base of the ornament. Insert the pick into the foam.

Floral foam is available in several shapes and sizes, including this 24" heart on a papier maché form used for the Floral Heart on page 106. Soak the entire form in water, and drain.

Foliage such as plumosa fern is used as a background and is placed into the base of the foam. Next, flowers—in this case, roses—are placed in the midline and carnations are used to fill in the top and down the sides. The form is completed by continuing around the shape, one section at a time.

Arrangements in Water

Before beginning, fill the container with lukewarm water almost to the top, allowing space for the stems. (Once the vase is arranged it is difficult to judge the correct amount of water to put in. Some flowers will also wilt if you take a long time to arrange them without water and their stem tips dry out, making it hard for them to take up water.)

For a free-form design, arrange flowers in hand and cut the bottoms of stems flush. Place flowers in the container and allow them to fall as they will and arrange themselves.

To position flowers in the center of a glass bowl or other wide-mouthed container, use a pin frog. Apply floral clay adhesive to the bottom of the pin frog and secure it to the bottom of the bowl. Cut the flowers to the desired length and place onto the pin frog. Cover the pin frog with colored marbles or pebbles and fill the bowl with water.

Gerbera daisies can be strengthened by using a stem sleeve, or floral tape and wire. The stem sleeve is slid over the stem of the flower to the base of the bloom to help the flower stand straight.

Floral tape and wire will allow some flexibility and stability of the stem. Insert a 21-gauge wire about ¼" into the bloom against the stem. Apply light green colored floral tape and wrap down the stem to the bottom of the wire.

A fresh flower pick can be used as an accent, as in the Ivy Topiary on page 113. Fill a water tube with lukewarm water. Place the main flower, such as this rose, in the center of the tube. Next, place filler flower, such as gypsophila, around the rose, making certain the stems are long enough to take the water from the bottom of the tube. The flower pick can be placed into a plant or other material as an accent.

Plastic Foam

Plastic foam is used for stabilizing props and flowers and foliage that can dry naturally in the arrangement. The Rice Bowl on page 129 is constructed by cutting a small piece of plastic foam to fit the bottom of the bowl. Place a roll of floral clay adhesive to the bottom of the plastic foam and secure to the bottom of the bowl. Fill the bowl with rice (or other material, i.e., seeds or beans). Insert the stem of a Cymbidium Orchid (or other flower) into a water tube and bury the tube in the rice, securing it into the plastic foam.

Wiring Flowers

Sturdy stems do not require wire to stand in an arrangement, but more fragile stems will require wiring. For roses, insert a 21-gauge wire approximately ¼" into the calyx and bloom, taking care to avoid the seed pod. Wind the wire down along the stem, around the foliage. Approximately 1" from the end of the stem, bend the wire back up toward the bloom and close it in around the stem.

To tape and wire a flower for a body flower, cut the flower stem to approximately 1". Insert a 12" length of 24-gauge wire through the stem, at the bottom of the bloom. Bend the wire down around the stem and wrap with floral tape. Add accents such as gypsophila or seeded eucalyptus next, wrapping a few stems at a time with floral tape.

Special Consideration

When working with any unfamiliar flower or foliage—especially exotic flowers, do your homework as to whether they require any special care. For example, the Bird of Paradise does not continue to open after it has been cut from the plant. The bloom must be removed from the calyx. First, soak the head of the flower in lukewarm water for 5–7 minutes. Starting at the back of the head, gently insert your thumb. Slide your thumb forward and force the blooms out of the flower. Remove the white membranes and separate the blooms until fully opened.

Out from the Garden

It is not only necessary to love, it is necessary to show that love.
—French Proverb

Flowers have carried messages, offered comfort, and confessed love throughout the ages. The Victorians were particularly well known for the subtle and sometimes complex meaning they bestowed, not only on each flower, but also on the manner it was presented.

Men and women used the beauty and brilliance of flowers to express a language of emotions and dreams they could not speak out loud.

Each bouquet, corsage, or simple cluster was carefully selected to represent the giver's precise meaning. The vocabulary was rich, each arrangement meaningful, and true love confessed without saying a word.

...and what more lovely, sweet, and thoughtful way to show love, any sort of love, than the gift of flowers?

Today, we have the wonderful joy of giving our most beloved flowers freely, for any reason or no reason at all. And remember, the container you place them in can have as much impact as the type of flower it holds. Do not limit yourself to the traditional crystal vase. Buckets, bowls, mugs, and bottles add character and charm. Even a wicker basket or a small, wooden crate can be lined to hold water and would make a warm and rustic home for your bouquets.

Say thank you to a friend by gathering a bunch of hydrangea and tying them with ribbon. Or, tell your dad hello with a bright arrangement of snapdragons, just because.

"Dear Andrea,
You have been a true friend and I thank you for it!
With all my love, a flower for you..."

These gifts from nature can be the most wonderful gifts of love!

Facing Page

Use plenty of flowers with thick, strong stems, such as these gladiolus, to fill the mouth of any tall container or vase, even a hollow column with a glass in the bottom to hold water. The result will be a simple but striking focal point of a room.

Right

Short-stemmed flowers such as these white Stargazer lilies will need the support of a frog or foam to arrange them beautifully in any short container such as this round blue bowl with an opening large enough to hold the lilies and lush foliage.

Flowers
Variegated Pink & White Gladiolus

Silver Dollar Eucalyptus
White Stargazer Lily

Right

Combining floral arangements of varied heights and shapes adds drama and interest to an otherwise ordinary staircase. This same technique would be equally extraordinary as a table centerpiece grouping or floor composition.

Facing Page Top

A round, black container filled with a combination of lilies, roses, and greenery, makes a romantic mix that focuses on the variety and color of the arrangement. Using a large cluster of flowers balances the size and width of the bowl.

Facing Page Bottom

Use the same type of round container to create a very different look. Choose any type of formal flower such as carnations or lilacs of the same color and cut the stems short for a look that is both classic and delicate.

Flowers

Isralia Ruscus
Virginia Rose

Calla Lily
Italian Ruscus
Steel Grass

Cut Green Ivy
Pink Oriental Lily
Virginia Rose

Salal (Lemon Leaf)
Vogue Rose

Left
These calla lilies, a celebration of purity and grace, need no other embellishment than a battenburg lace handkerchief tied with a gossamer ribbon or piece of natural twine.

Facing Page
Any tall, cylindrical container, bottle, or vase would be perfect for the linear, strong-stemmed calla lily. Just take care that any pattern or design on the container does not compete with the drama of the lilies. The addition of the foliage softens the look of the display.

God gave angels wings, and humans flowers. These calla lilies,
a celebration of beauty, purity of heart, and all things heavenly,
would make even angels envy these humans.

Can you imagine
a more glorious
"welcome home"
than these calla lilies
waiting in your
friend's entry?

People from a planet
without flowers
would think we must
be mad with joy...
to have such things about us.
—Iris Murdoch

31

The V-shaped vase draws the eye upward to an armful of white and red roses and salal. The rose stems are reinforced with wire and green floral tape, maintaining the strength of the rose and the shape of the arrangement.

The red rose whispers
of passion,
And the white rose
breathes of love;
O, the red rose
is a falcon,
And the white rose
is a dove.
—John Boyle O' Reilly

...and the vibrant
combination of white
and red together
in a rose signifies unity.

Flowers
Hybrid Delphinium
Italian Ruscus
Pink Oriental Lily
Pink Snapdragon

Such a wide combination of flowers in such varied shapes, heights, and textures could seem disorderly. However, in this layered arrangement the delicate, subtle shades of blue, purple, and pink set atop unadorned dark green foliage blend to create a pleasing bouquet that looks just-picked from an English garden. Any assortment of flowers in hues of the same color will look harmonious and polished.

Flowers
Blue Agapanthus
Italian Ruscus
Pink Hydrangea
Silver Dollar Eucalyptus

Hybrid Delphinium
Pink Hydrangea

Left
Pink hydrangea blooms and silver dollar ruscus fill a sleek cylinder and act as a support for the tall playful agapanthus. Add as many stems as necessary to fill the space where the arrangement will be placed.

Facing Page
Blooms with stems too short to be in an arrangement can still make a statement. Here, pink hydrangea and violet delphinium garnish an heirloom plate.

For in each one of them one would be confronted by a miracle—
the miracle that so tiny a thing should hold in its core the perfume of eternity.
—Beverly Nichols

Flowers
Blue Agapanthus
Gerbera Daisy
Italian Ruscus

Italian Ruscus
Pink Oriental Lily

Top
The warm and friendly gerbera daisy stems are wired and wrapped and anchored in place by the two stems of agapanthus at the mouth of the clear, azure blue bowl. For a different look, try an old wooden box lined with plastic to hold the water or a glass jar tied with raffia and hanging wooden ornaments.

Bottom
The exotic pink oriental lilies are in full glory atop the sleek, bowl that sets off the accents of this modern kitchen. Cut the lily stems at varied lengths and place them one at a time in a crisscross pattern to build a stable composition of distinct shape.

Flowers
White Stargazer Lily

For an easy but breathtaking arrangement, choose a bouquet of one single type of flower that is unusual and unique in shape. The exquisite design and splendor of the white stargazer lily requires no other ornamentation but a container tall enough to support their willowy height.

Petals of Paradise

Need an escape from your ordinary day-to-day routine? Or perhaps you have a coworker that you have caught staring off into space at their "Tropical Islands of the World" calendar. A gift of flowers, either for yourself or a friend, is the closest thing to the pleasure of a physical escape. Here you will find tropical blooms to warm and awaken, with colors dipped from an imagined tropical sunset. Far beyond the ordinary, the fragrances and textures of these exotic flowers will delight and surprise. A thoughtful gift like these unusual arrangements will have the power to transport and transform.

Need to book a larger group getaway? Turn an ordinary summer evening into a memorable escape for you and your friends. Many of the flowers used in this chapter are native to tropical islands and exotic paradises. They will bring with them the color and excitement of their homelands. Such brilliant colors and varied textures can stand alone as striking centerpieces and side-table arrangements. Use the flowers to create an exotic mood that you can expand upon with anything from oil-burning tiki torches to experimenting with a multicultural recipe.

Feel free to simplify the larger, lush arrangements into smaller, less expensive versions. Or create one large composition for the grand banquet table, then use a single bloom in a small wooden bowl on each guest table to complement the overall theme.

If these exotic flowers are not available in your area, there are many variations on these designs that would be equally stunning. In place of the Bird of Paradise, you could use any tall vibrant flower such as the tiger lily. No bamboo tiki torches handy? There are many creative candles with exotic, bamboo-like textures that could be used to illuminate a beautiful arrangement.

The height and scale of some of these tropical flowers and their heavy stems require a durable and weighty container, perhaps pottery or stone. Don't be afraid to choose bold containers for these lush arrangements. In addition, think of your creations in levels. Start with the main dramatic bloom and work out and down to smaller flowers near the bottom, adding balance and interest. Following a few simple principles will allow you to create fantastic compositions.

Let your imagination fly like the Birds of Paradise that grace these pages. Be inspired by the lively tropical colors, fragrances, and textures of these exciting flowers. Anything you create will surely be memorable.

Flowers

Bird of Paradise
Curly Willow
Honeycomb Heliconia
Hypericum
Italian Ruscus
Pink Anthurium
Pink Frost Protea
Pink Ginger
Salal (Lemon Leaf)
Steel Grass
Ti Foliage

Begin this array with the pink ginger and bird of paradise. Scale the design down to the protea which adds weight and becomes the focal point. The mixture of foliage and other flowers added to the sides frames the design and provides a visual effect of color and texture.

Flowers

Bamboo
Banksia Protea
Bird of Paradise
Croton Foliage
Heliconia
Monstera Foliage
Pink Frost Protea
Red Anthurium
Seeded Eucalyptus
Ti Foliage

Everything here works around the striking heliconia. Bamboo adds height. Red anthurium provides color and balance. Birds of Paradise frame the heliconia on each side. Finally, foliage and protea hide the supporting floral foam at the base of the arrangement.

My gift to you, my friend, is a warm, wild heaven. Flowers blazing like fire, suns, and rainbows.
Emerald and sunshine leaves spotted like a parrot's feathers. Foliage you cannot help but touch.
Creation romancing you in the voice of a thousand birds.

Flowers

Gnarly Branch

Hypericum

Monstera Foliage

Pink Frost Protea

Purple Dendrobium Orchid

Red Anthurium

Reindeer Moss

Seeded Eucalyptus

Ti Foliage

Looking as though it may have evolved organically on its own, this dense grouping begins with a heavy bowl. Ti leaves and monstera foliage form the shape of the arrangement, with a gnarly branch for added intrigue. Anthurium, dendrobium orchids, and mosses surround and draw attention to the four pink frost protea.

What a thoughtful
and unforgettable
housewarming present!
Glass anthurium joined
with living Bird of Paradise
and Italian ruscus before
the mirror's reflection will
welcome a new couple
to what may be an empty
new home, with a gift of
brilliance and color.

A crystal vase. A plastic cube. A ceramic planter. A stoneware mug.
Can it hold water? Then it can be a creative way to display flowers! Fill a clear
container with polished rocks, shells, colored beads or buttons, coins, or tiny knick-
knacks and you have a gift to be used after the blossoms have faded.

<u>Flowers</u>

Bamboo	Hypericum
Bird of Paradise	Pink Frost Protea
Croton Foliage	Purple Dendrobium Orchid
Honeycomb Heliconia	Seeded Eucalyptus

For a centerpiece that is spectacular from any standpoint, bunch Bird of Paradise of the same height with all heads facing outward. Bind these up with raffia and center them in floral foam. Landscape all around with varying levels of flowers and foliage.

Flowers

Bamboo

Pin Cushion Protea

Bird of Paradise

Croton Foliage

Hypericum

Italian Ruscus

Monstera Foliage

Oncidium Orchid

Reindeer Moss

Salal (Lemon Leaf)

Steel Grass

Ti Foliage

Flowers
Croton Foliage

Curly Willow

Dracena Foliage

Honeycomb Heliconia

Oncidium Orchid

Pink Ginger

Red Anthurium

Steel Grass

Facing Page

Exotic Bird of Paradise stems define the height of this arrangement while sturdy bamboo and Ti leaves build the framework. Pincushion protea and oncidium orchids give focus, movement, and vibrant color. It is finished with moss and hypericum for enticing tropical texture.

Right

This natural, free-form creation rises up from a water-filled container. Meandering curly willow acts as a support for the other flowers. The orchid stems accentuate the willow's flow and curves. When building the levels, use ginger for height, heliconia in the middle, and anthurium near the bottom.

Orchids that speak of love and beauty. The Red Ginger talks of strength. Coconuts suggest abundance. Pineapples communicate good luck. Bamboo brings you peace. You are surrounded by tiki torches burning exotic scented oils. Here you may breathe calmly, relax, and share a twilight dinner with a good friend.

Flowers

Coconut

Croton Foliage

Flowering Artichoke

Heliconia

Monstera Foliage

Oncidium Orchid

Pineapple

Purple Dendrobium Orchid

Red Anthurium

Red Ginger

This fiery outdoor composition, with tiki torches of varied heights, will be the hit of your next outdoor party. Use the torches to prop up each descending level of blooms; first heliconia, then ginger. Add the orchids and anthurium for width and balance. Finally the exotic and robust gathering of pineapple, artichokes, and coconuts give interest, appeal, and texture that echoes the woven torches.

Flowers

Bamboo
Banksia Protea
Curly Willow
Hanging Heliconia
Monstera Foliage

Place bamboo, harbinger of peace and luck, in plastic foam. Monstera foliage adds width with banksia protea on top. Hanging heliconia among it all offers striking color and drama.

Summer Wild Flowers

The Greek sun god Apollo drove his shining chariot from East to West across the sky, bringing with him the glorious sunshine. Each day as he drove, Clytie, a sweet mortal woman who loved him, longed for her fair Apollo. But he did not

return her love. Yet she remained faithful, eventually dying of her unrequited love.

Aphrodite, goddess of love, had been watching poor Clytie and was so impressed by her devotion to Apollo, that she turned Clytie into a beautiful flower, with sunshine yellow blossoms and a strong root.

Now, as Apollo continues to drive his chariot across the sky, the devoted face of the sunflower's blossom turns to follow his journey.

Because the sunflower turns to follow the sun, it has come to symbolize loyalty, devotion, and constancy. The Chinese believe it to be a symbol of longevity. The native Plains Indians of North America held the sunflower in esteem and used its seeds as a sacred food in ceremonies. Ancient South American cultures used the flower in worship, hammering images of the Sunflower into gold to be worn by priests and priestesses and hung in their temples.

Today, the bright sunflower is still beloved. The joy of these arrangements is their versatility. These earthy designs invite your own creative ways of using original props and containers, such as a birdhouse or worn watering can. The foliage selected for these arrangements could easily be replaced with other green or dried plants, even those from your own back yard. The flowers and fruits will dry naturally, ensuring you a charming and long-lasting decoration or gift. The delightful additions and containers can then be saved and reused as a remembrance of that special party or your thoughtful gift. In any arrangement, the sunflower will bring with it the warmth, love, and devotion it symbolizes, just as its sunny, round, blooms recall the circular journey of Apollo across the sky.

Flowers
Artichoke
Bells of Ireland
Cattail
Italian Ruscus
Spiral Eucalyptus
Sunflower

Cattails provide height and the sunflowers create circular motion of design. The foliage not only adds depth but also secures the other stems. The surprising ornamental artichokes were wired together and tied to the bucket's handle with raffia.

This reflective gazing ball, thought to attract fairies and good luck, is secured with a plant stick into floral foam with the fruit and flowers tucked tightly around it.

Flowers

Artichoke   Purple Statice

Italian Ruscus   Sunflower

Lime

Flowers

Artichoke

Cattail

Gold Yarrow

Isralia Ruscus

Lime

Potted Green Ivy

Purple Statice

Sunflower

Artichoke

Cattail

Equisetum

Gold Yarrow

Hypericum

Italian Ruscus

Lime

Purple Statice

Salal (Lemon Leaf)

Sunflower

Levels and detail make this arrangement special. Cattails tower above the purchased birdhouse and sunflowers placed at varied heights. All are nestled in a bed of ivy.

The bottoms of these artichokes were sliced off so they would sit level and the insides removed to hold small and fragrant votive candles.

The heart that has truly loved never forgets,
But as truly loves on to the close,
As the sunflower turns on her god when he sets
The same look that she turned when he rose.
—Moore

But friendship is precious, not only in the shade, but in the sunshine of life;
and thanks to a benevolent arrangement of things, the greater part of life is sunshine.
—Thomas Jefferson

<u>*Flowers*</u>
Artichoke
Cattail
Gold Yarrow
Italian Ruscus
Lime
Purple Statice
Spanish Moss
Steel Grass
Sunflower

Nearly any type of flower can be used for this clustered look held in florist's foam. Sturdy stems can stand on their own while more fragile stems need the help of wire. Band the stems by wrapping them with raffia in a crisscross fashion for a braided look.

Something as simple as bending two stems of equisetum at different levels creates an unexpected visual effect. Asparagus could be substituted for a similar look in a low arrangement.

Flowers

Artichoke	Equisetum
Equisetum	Salal (Lemon Leaf)
Salal (Lemon Leaf)	Seed Ball
Spanish Moss	Spanish Moss
Sunflower	Sunflower

This display is perfect for an outdoor patio. Each container is filled with plastic foam and the bottom is glued to the foam in the previous container. Bonus! Everything in it is dried. No watering or upkeep!

Flowers
Artichoke
Gold Yarrow
Italian Ruscus
Lime
Purple Statice
Spanish Moss
Sunflower

For best results, use a sturdy stemmed flower for this look. Band top cluster with raffia, add second cluster around stems of the first, and wrap all stems as one. Repeat for the third and fourth clusters until all are connected.

Flowers

Artichoke

Gold Yarrow

Isralia Ruscus

Lime

Purple Statice

Spanish Moss

Sunflower

Flowers

Artichoke

Cattail

Potted Green Ivy

Steel Grass

Sunflower

When is a container not a container? When it is a wall hanging disguising the foam-based arrangement behind it. More flowers and artichokes were added to the front with floral adhesive.

For an array that delights from any angle, place each blossom facing a different direction and tightly fill in the entire circumference of the base.

Flowers
Artichoke
Isralia Ruscus
Italian Ruscus
Spanish Moss
Sunflower

Artichoke
Italian Ruscus
Purple Statice

Equisetum
Gold Yarrow

Harvest Blossoms

For the hay and the corn and the wheat that is reaped,
For the labor well done, and the barns that are heaped,
For the sun and the dew and the sweet honeycomb,
For the rose and the song and the harvest brought home.
—Author unknown

However, in this season, with so much to be thankful for and so many reasons for giving flowers, be careful not to neglect the other delights of nature that make autumn so alive with vibrant textures and colors.

Changing leaves, gourds and pumpkins, stalks of wheat, dried seed pods, ripe vegetables from your garden (or the supermarket), all can be added to the already brilliant golds, oranges, and reds of your flowers.

Let your imagination overflow like a cornucopia! Combine flowers and veggies, leaves and stalks to create inviting gifts or centerpieces for any type of fall celebration.

What words would you use now to describe the Thanksgiving celebrations of your childhood?

Or did you not think of autumn as a time of flowers? In the wake of the other seasons, it could be easy to overlook the blossoming abundance that surrounds us at this time of year. Many roses and other flowers are at their most beautiful in late summer and early fall.

Warm, homey, abundant, full of a rich mixture of things that delight the senses— things to see and smell and touch and taste. Baskets over-flowing with the fruits of a long year's labor.

Keep these images and memories in mind as you think of ways to express your love and gratitude to your friends and loved ones.

The amber light of fall hangs over harvested fields, brown hues of turned earth. The scent of fallen apples, the sharp, gentle chill. Here as we move into the Autumn, the glorious sunset before the morning of spring, let the lord of the harvest teach us gratitude for all nature's gifts, and for one another.

　　　—Autumn Equinox Ritual

Flowers

Ambiance Rose
Confetti Rose
Lotus Pod
Mini Pumpkin
Orange Enchantment Lily
Seeded Eucalyptus

Pepper
Spanish Moss

Bread
Lotus Pod

Nesting baskets were used in this display. The two smaller baskets are tightly packed with peppers and bread. Moss and foliage were added for texture and lotus pods were glued right onto the smallest baskets. You could substitute any seasonal produce to create many different moods.

The juxtaposition of velvety soft roses among seed pods and pumpkins adds interest and elegance to a colorful centerpiece in a brilliant season.

Any type of gourd, squash, or pumpkin can be used as an ornament to add rich appeal to any arrangement. Just add a floral pick!

By all these lovely tokens / September days are here,
With summer's best of weather / And autumn's best of cheer.
—Author Unknown

Try echoing the motifs on a container as you construct your bouquet, such as the fruit on these kitchen canisters. Any type of fruit, vegetable, or plant in season can be combined with beautiful blossoms. Just keep complementary themes and colors in mind.

Flowers

Cattail Stem	Cattail	Cattail Top
Green Ivy	Confetti Rose	Confetti Rose
Plum	Green Ivy	Green Ivy
Purple Statice	Hypericum	Hypericum
	Nectarine	Nectarine

Flowers
Bread
Dried Pomegranate
Hypericum
Italian Ruscus
Potted Yellow Kalanchoe Plant
Red Gerbera Daisy
Steel Grass
Dried Wheat
White Grape

Hypericum
Mini Red Gerbera Daisy
White Grape

In place of flowers, bread was sliced and added to the design. Potted plants were tucked inside the oblong container and flowers and wheat were tied with raffia and secured in floral foam.

The bread bowl filled with a single gerbera daisy and bunches of white grapes and hypericum makes for an intriguing side arrangement.

Flowers

African Violet	Mini Pumpkin
Breadstick	Pepper
Bronze Chrysanthemum	Salal (Lemon Leaf)
Dried Wheat	Tangerine Carnation
Hypericum	Yellow Marigold
Italian Ruscus	Yellow Viking Pompon
Mini Gourd	

A wooden salad set was the inspiration for this table grouping. Wheat stalks were turned horizontally to create length and visually connect the smaller satellite arrangements. You could also use kitchen gadgets, cookies, crackers, or candies to fill the bowls. Anything is possible!

To Autumn:

All the daughters of the year shall dance!

Sing now the lusty song of fruits and flowers!

—Blake

A beautiful wooden bowl, overflowing with breadsticks, and nestled with simple touches of the season,
will transform easily from a welcomed hostess gift, to the centerpiece for a buffet table's feast!

This abundant harvest array begins with a purchased grapevine wreath lying on the table. Silk and fresh flowers were then inserted into the wreath. The pheasant stands on its own to the side. The fresh flowers will dry beautifully for a delightfully long-lasting arrangement.

Flowers

Artichoke

Bells of Ireland

Bronze Chrysanthemum

Dried Wheat

Eggplant

Gourd

Hypericum

Italian Ruscus

Mini Pumpkin

Salal (Lemon Leaf)

Seeded Eucalyptus

Silk African Violet

Silk Oncidium Orchid

Silk Red Cabbage

Yellow Gerbera Daisy

Ere, in the
northern gale,
The summer tresses
of all the trees are gone,
The woods of Autumn,
all around our vale,
Have put
their glory on.
—William Cullen Bryant

Delicious autumn!
My very soul
is wedded to it, and
if I were a bird
I would fly
about the earth
seeking the successive
autumns.
—George Eliot

Flowers

Gold Carnation
Hypericum

Bells of Ireland
Broccoflower
Brussel Sprout
Confetti Rose
Hypericum
Italian Ruscus
Leoniedas Rose
Versilia Rose

Hypericum
Italian Ruscus
Leoniedas Rose
Yellow Viking Pompon

Broccoflower
Brussel Sprout
Cattail
Hypericum
Italian Ruscus

Ceramic containers shaped like fruits and vegetables make fun and unique settings for any combination of flowers and veggies such as cauliflower, small potatoes, or brussel sprouts.

Lush, full, flowers look abundant and romantic tucked into organic containers.
Combining your favorite treasured flowers in the vibrant rich colors of autumn
along with other gifts from nature's harvest will create a look that is both elegant and robust.

Arrange flowers in the baskets you gathered them in! The flowers are set in floral foam and the bread is picked into plastic foam for stability.

Of all the gifts that wise Providence grants us to make life full and happy, friendship is the most beautiful.
—*Epicurus*

Flowers

Confetti Rose	Lotus Pod	Yellow Gerbera Daisy
Dried Wheat	Orange Gerbera Daisy	Seeded Eucalyptus
Hypericum	Pink Frost Protea	Tangerine Carnation
Italian Ruscus		

This arrangement may look difficult, but is very easily made. Flowers, pods, and veggies are set with picks into a floral foam ring. This can then be set on top of an iron bowl as shown, or encircling the base of a punch bowl.

Flowers

Hypericum	Mini Pumpkin	Seed Ball
Gourd	Orange Enchantment Lily	Seeded Eucalyptus
Leoniedas Rose	Orange Gerbera Daisy	Yellow Pompon Daisy
Lotus Pod		

Christmas in Bloom

Snow has settled on rooftops and candlelight glimmers and lights the faces of expectant children. Dinner is presented on the good china, Bing Crosby croons from the massive corner radio, and the potent scent of carefully placed pine boughs fills the air. All set the stage for a memorable holiday.

In this enchanted season, ways and reasons to give flowers are as plentiful as a child's list for presents. When visiting your florist, you may be surprised at the amount and variety of flowers available in the winter months. Let the bright, rich colors of the winter blooms combine with plenty of thick inviting mixtures of greenery. Holiday arrangements can range from something delicate and simple to a grand and lush decoration that will be the center of attention.

As you give, keep in mind that these flowers of the winter holidays are some of the most meaningful and symbolic of the year. The holly tree was known to medieval monks as the "Holy Tree" because it was believed to keep evil spirits away and protect the home. It eventually became a Christian symbol for eternal life. When placed in a house before Christmas Eve and removed the day after Christmas it is said to bless the home with domestic happiness. The vibrant poinsettia, in white, pink, and red is used to decorate churches and homes and brings with it wishes of mirth and celebration.

Once again you scan your gift list. How many of those impossible-to-buy-for people are there? What do you give the friend who has everything? The unforgettable and intimate gift of her favorite flowers, beribboned and bowed in the jeweled tones of burgundy and green.

Gifts of flowers need not be large or extravagant to be special, thoughtful, and memorable. The table setting for a traditional holiday dinner is made complete with floral touches. Float a deep red rose bud in a small, dime-store glass bowl. Using a gold marker, write the name of each guest on the front of each bowl for polished place cards they can take home.

Purchased poinsettias can be repotted in a wonderful basket that can be reused or in that special piece of pottery that was made by a grandchild.

Small, winter bouquets are just right to show appreciation for a special babysitter, school teacher, or store clerk who always offers a smile and a sincere wish for a nice day.

At right, gardenias were placed on the tree to be given as hostess gifts to guests as they depart. Place the stem of each flower in a small water tube and wire it to the tree. Roses, lilies, or orchids could also be used this way to make your next holiday party special.

Our hearts they hold all Christmas dear,
And earth seems sweet and heaven seems near.
                                        —Marjorie L. C. Pickthall

Flowers

Gardenia   Silk Rose

Flowers
Burgundy Carnation
Charlotte Rose
Green Hydrangea
Potted Ivy Plant

Jolly plush Santas take a moment to relax from the holiday rush in a wicker chair among fragrant flowers and potted ivy. Bears, dolls, or toys would be equally charming here.

Left

Purchased Santas with a ring at the back were spruced up and used as napkin rings and candleholders.

Right

Roses and gypsophila pose as tree ornaments and heather inserted at the base of each topiary forms a natural tree skirt.

Flowers

Cedar

Hypericum

Ming Fern

Red Carnation

Snowberry

Green Ivy Topiary Plant

Million Star Gypsophila

Heather

Sahara Rose

Left
Fill a glass container with a variety of fruit —sliced, shaped, or whole. Add vinegar to preserve the fruit.

Right
Christmas ornaments can hold water too. Any hollow holiday ornament can be used as a vase just waiting for floral adornment.

Christmas has come; let every man
...be merry all he can.
...No matter what lies in the bowls,
We'll make it rich with our own souls.
—William Henry Davies

Flowers

Charlotte Rose
Gardenia
Lemon

Lime
Oncidium Orchid
Orange

Flowers

Charlotte Rose

Green Hydrangea

Italian Ruscus

Pine Wreath

Red Carnation

Seeded Eucalyptus

Snowberry

Wax Flower

White Daisy Pompon

Top

Feel free to add, mix, and match fresh, dried, and artificial blooms to a seasonal green wreath.

Bottom

For a sweet decoration, glue three candy peppermints in a circle and add a daisy pompon to the center. White daisies were also attached to the base of each festively colored taper candle.

The Love of Roses

Where'er you tread,
the blushing flowers will rise,
And all things flourish
where you turn your eyes.
—Alexander Pope

What could be more romantic than flowers? And roses are the most romantic blooms of all. But the important thing to realize about roses and the other flowers that grace this chapter is, while often used to form glorious classic and formal arrangements, they can be used for so much more!

Nothing is more classic than a dozen long-stemmed red roses in a crystal vase for Valentine's Day. But how about dividing up a dozen roses, easily purchased at the local supermarket, tying each with a silky ribbon and a small tag. Write on each tag one trait you love about your sweetheart, then leave each rose at twelve different places where he or she will find them throughout the day. (Be sure to place each in a little water tube so they won't die of thirst!)

You can change the entire mood of a bouquet of roses simply by changing the flowers that fill in among them. Carnations or baby's breath are traditional and give a very formal feeling. However, fill in around those same lovely long-stemmed roses with dried, curvy twigs or grasses, and you have a look that is warm and more casual.

You also can change the look from formal to casual by your choice of containers. Of course, roses and carnations look elegant and sublime in sparkling crystal or sterling silver; but they can look inviting and touchable as a bouquet lying in a gathering basket adorned with seashells or tucked into a loosely gathered wreath around a punch bowl.

Make your guests feel especially welcome by gracing fluffy white bathroom towels with a couple of blossoms tied with a grosgrain bow. Or place a sweet, pink rosebud and velvety rose petals on their pillow.

Scatter fresh rose petals across your beautifully laid dining table, then place a single bud in a small bud vase or even a china teacup, by the setting for each guest. Get especially intimate by choosing the color of each bud to match the personality of each guest. It's these little details that are so thoughtful and memorable.

Wrapping a gift? Replace those prepackaged sticky bows with a miniature bouquet tied to the package with ribbon or twine. Uncertain of what to give? Put together an indulgent care basket complete with bubble bath, rose scented lotions or powders, a CD of soft music, and a tissue-paper bag filled with rose petals to be sprinkled in the bath water. What better way to soothe the soul than by bathing in roses!

Now that roses and other flowers are so readily available and often quite inexpensive, especially if you arrange them yourself, there is simply no reason not to fill your life and the lives of your loved ones with flowers!

Flowers

Bluebird Rose

Charlotte Rose

Green Ivy Plant

Ravel Rose

Vogue Rose

An ivy plant fills the base of this ceramic swan, while an abundance of roses is wired for strength and tucked tightly together in floral foam to make up the body of the swan.

103

Flowers
Million Star Gypsophila
Ravel Rose
Vogue Rose

Gardenia
Pink Renata Rose
Plumosa Fern

Ravel Rose

A collection of crystal containers makes a lovely and romantic grouping. A ring of floral foam covered with roses and gardenias surrounds a bowl. Add a perfumed floating candle for ambiance.

Float gardenias and single petals in a crystal bowl,

and in moments you have a spot that is soft, serene, and romantic.

We bring roses, beautiful fresh roses, / Dewy as the morning and colored like the dawn.

—Thomas Buchanan Read

Left
Select a whimsical porcelain statuette or resin figurine to embellish with flowers.

Facing Page Top
Individual nosegays made in tussy mussy holders and a sprinkling of single petals surround an elegantly simple cake.

Facing Page Bottom Left
Fill any bowl with fresh blooms from your garden.

Flowers
Pink Nora Carnation
Ravel Rose
Plumosa Fern

Queen Anne's Lace
Pink Renata Rose
Plumosa Fern

Bluebird Rose
Plumosa Fern

White Mini Carnation

Charlotte Rose
Queen Anne's Lace

...(i do not know what it is about you that closes and opens; only something

in me understands the voice of your eyes is deeper than all roses)...

—e.e. cummings

<u>*Flowers*</u>

Charlotte Rose
Pink Renata Rose
Plumosa Fern
Vogue Rose
White Calycina

Charlotte Rose
Million Star Gypsophila

Million Star Gypsophila
Vogue Rose

Facing Page
Here, plumosa fern creates a shadowing waterfall effect over the roses.

Left
Create fanciful topiaries from roses by wiring the stems for strength and standing them very closely together in a container filled with floral foam. Finish with a blooming garland at the base.

109

Express sympathy with
a cluster of warm pink roses
tucked into a silver sugar
bowl. Give dark pink roses
to a thoughtful friend to show
your gratitude. Or place a
pale pink bud lovingly on
her pillow to express the joy
your heart feels, just because
she is your daughter.

What if you slept?
And what if,
in your sleep
you dreamed?
And what if,
in your dream,
you went to heaven
and there plucked a
[moon colored] flower?
And what if,
when you awoke,
you had the flower
in your hand?
—Samuel Taylor Coleridge

Left
Continue the woven pattern of the charming white basket with short-stemmed roses and sweet violets placed in tight, alternating rows.

Facing Page
Create a romantic mood with topiary trees embellished with rose blooms and potted African violets. Soften the spheres and create a Victorian look with sheer flowing ribbons and gypsophila.

Flowers

Charlotte Rose	Million Star Gypsophila
Pink Renata Rose	Pink Renata Rose
Potted Mini African Violet	Potted African Violet
Ravel Rose	Potted Ivy Topiary Plant

Designer Whites

Flowers…have a mysterious and subtle
influence upon the feelings,
not unlike some strains of music,
they relax the tenseness of the mind.
                    —Henry Ward Beecher

And what better flowers to bring peace and help relieve the days cares, than blossoms washed in the hues of angel's wings? The refined grace and purity of flowers all in white is comfortable in any setting, from formal lilies in crystal vases to friendly snapdragons bunched together with tall grasses.

When the color is understated, our focus then moves to often overlooked characteristics, such as the shape of the petals, the curve of a stem, the delicate container, a crisp, clear fragrance. The wonderful reward of working with white is how easy it is to create a fresh and elegant arrangement. Depending on the container you choose, a grouping of gorgeous, white flowers in a straight glass cylinder can accent the top of a friend's sleek black piano, or fill a wicker basket on your aunt's coffee table.

Choose luxurious white blooms to convey a heart full of meanings. Give a gift of pale cream orchids to thank your mother for a lifetime of wisdom and thoughtfulness. Send your best friend an armful of flawless calla lilies the week before her wedding as a reflection of her beauty, and the joy and hope in her new life to come. Snowy white French tulips have long been used as a first declaration of pure and perfect love to either a man or a woman.

Never thought of sending flowers to a man? A subdued white gathering of sophisticated blooms mixed with natural branches, stalks, grasses, or eucalyptus will make a polished arrangement that he will never forget!

Snowy bits of unblemished light, these flowers, have been placed here for our enjoyment and love! Share their pristine beauty with those you know, and fill your own home and surroundings with the peace these flowers bring. Straightforward and pure—allow flowers to arrange themselves by placing them in a water-filled vase and letting them fall as they will. Select them when they are yet buds and watch the composition change as the flowers come to bloom.

Give a loving gift to yourself by creating a harmonious space of your own to read or meditate. A cushiony chair to sink into, a fragrant ivory candle, and a single white gardenia floating in a small glass bowl. Simplicity always makes a bold statement.

Facing Page

Bunches of steel grass were placed on a pin frog in water and surrounded by exotic glass ornaments. White eskimo rosebuds float closely together in a nearby crystal bowl.

Left and Right Bottom

For a sleek, sculpted appearance, warm each stem to bend in your hands. Place calla lilies together in a vase and tulip blooms in a bowl with a bit of water.

Flowers

Steel Grass   Calla Lily   White Eskimo Rose   White French Tulip
White Eskimo Rose

<u>Flowers</u>
Gardenia

White Anthurium

Left
Crystal candleholders in this cabinet were filled with a different type of light—intoxicating white gardenias.

Above
Something as simple as varying the water level adds intrigue to this trio of anthurium blooms in identical vases.

<u>Flowers</u>

White French Tulips	*Calla Lily*	*Cymbidium Orchid*
White Snapdragons	*Gardenia*	*White Anthurium*

Facing Page
Unpretentious, classical, refined. White tulips and snapdragons are abundant and unassuming.

Left
Calla lilies, candles, and gardenias create a pristine center of illumination and fragrance.

Right
Unblemished white anthurium and cymbidium orchids repose in harmony.

The Art of Asian

Flowers reflect the human search for meaning. Does not each of us, ache to have a life as beautiful and true to itself as that of a flower?

—Phillip Moffitt

In ancient Japan, respect, understatement, and grace were integral parts of the culture. Often what polite refinement could not say, was conveyed in other ways, such as music, poetry, and very often the mystical language of flowers. In the royal court of Japan, a suitor could be beloved or rejected, a friend could be comforted, or a loved one could be attended on their journey from this world into the next, with a carefully composed bouquet of flowers.

Aside from the unalterable circumstance of inherited family rank, successful display of aesthetic sensibility was the primary means of establishing personal distinction among members of the court, both male and female. The skills, subtle judgement, and taste demonstrated in the mixing of incense, the layering of patterned silk kimonos, musical performance, dance, [the styling of flowers, and writing of poetry], figured greatly both in one's appeal as a prospective romantic partner and in one's prospects for official advancement.

—Jane Hirshfield, "The Ink Dark Moon"

And such a rich and elegant vocabulary exists within the blooms and forms of these oriental creations! The stately and precious orchid, in its many forms, speaks of love, beauty, refinement, and thoughtfulness. The elegant acacia whispers of secret loves and friendships. The simple and calming moss holds in its soft texture some of the purest forms of love, charity, and the love of a mother. The yarrow is said to know the cure to an aching heart. Thank a dear friend for her understanding heart with the beautiful hydrangea. The strong stalks of the bamboo plant are known in ancient tradition to bring good luck

to any household that displays them. And, eternally, the white lily has spoken silently of majesty, honor, and the purity of the human heart.

Even if the recipient of any of these graceful arrangements is not fluent in the precise meanings, they will no doubt understand the love, thoughtfulness, and peace that these extraordinary flowers can bring to any space. The originality of these bouquets and arrangements is due, not only to the exotic beauty of the flowers and stems used in them, but to the grace, tender elegance, and peaceful sense of balance of each gathering. This harmonious simplicity, combined with the individual, breathtaking loveliness of these flowers, will allow you to freely use your imagination and creative ideas, to create unforgettable gifts of beauty and peace for not only your friends and loved ones, but for your own home as well.

Arranging a bowl of flowers in the morning can give a sense of quiet in a crowded day—like writing a poem, or saying a prayer.

—Anne Morrow Lindberg

Flowers
Bamboo Trellis bound with Raffia
String of Hearts
Yellow Oncidium Orchid

This striking and vibrant design, set on a sofa table, was specifically designed and placed to frame the unique artwork behind it. The bamboo trellis acts as a grid to hold the yellow oncidium orchids in place.

Facing Page
Grapevine, softened by soaking it in water and refrigerating it overnight, was reformed to create shapes that provide movement and expression to these paired arrangements.

Right
Like exploding fireworks or a mighty water fountain, large amounts of steel grass burst forth from the center of this grouping of orchids, protea, yarrow, and foliage.

Flowers

Dried Grapevine

German Statice

Italian Ruscus

Pink Hydrangea

Sanseveria Leaves

Variegated Lavender Dendrobium Orchid

Anthurium Foliage

Gold Yarrow

Italian Ruscus

Pink Frost Protea

Steel Grass

Variegated Purple Dendrobium Orchid

Yellow Oncidium Orchid

<u>Flowers</u>
German Statice
Guzmania Bettina Bromeliad Plant
Italian Ruscus
Mossy Branch
Pink Hydrangea
White Dendrobium Orchid
White Phalaenopsis Orchid Plant

Left
Orchid and bromeliad plants were combined with fresh flowers and foliage in this stunning centerpiece.

Facing Page
An uncommon use for some common items. These exquisite orchids are placed among chopsticks and rice.

More fragrant / because of the one
who saw and picked them, / these flowers, / precious, transient—
—Izumi Shikibu (trans. by Jane Hirshfield)

Flowers

Bamboo Trellis bound with Raffia

Purple Phalaenopsis Orchid Plant

White Phalaenopsis Orchid Plant

Three potted orchids, one arrangement.
Bamboo stalks tied with natural raffia
create unity and form.

Equisetum gives horizontal visual motion in each of these arrangements. The trellis, created by banding two bunches of equisetum together horizontally and attaching them to the two bunches rising up from the planter, adds vertical interest as well.

The dewdrop
on an orchid petal
clings long:
these petals,
pillars of your strength
made visible.
This dewdrop,
holding your jeweled image
in its orb.

Flowers

Equisetum	Equisetum
Hypericum	Hypericum
Spanish Moss	Italian Ruscus
Yellow Oncidium Orchid	Razor Blade Acacia
White Phalaenopsis Orchid Plant	Yellow Oncidium Orchid
	White Japhet Orchid

<u>Flowers</u>
Curly Willow

Flax

German Statice

Italian Ruscus

Variegated Lavender Dendrobium Orchid

White Stargazer Lily

Yellow Oncidium Orchid

For an exotic Asian effect, willow branches were cut and pruned and combined with flax, which communicates a sense of oneness. Other branches, such as plum or cherry, could also be used in this manner.

*Glossary
of Flowers*

Flowers
AFRICAN VIOLET
Blue
Faithfulness

AGAPANTHUS
White, blue, and
lavender

ANTHURIUM
Red, white, pink,
orange, and
variegated shades

BELLS OF
IRELAND
Pale to medium green
Good Luck

BIRD OF PARADISE
Orange/blue
Strange and Wonderful

CALLA LILY
White, pink, and
yellow
Magnificent Beauty

CALYCINA
White

CARNATION
White, pink, peach,
red, yellow, and
variegated shades
Fascination, Devotion

CHRYSANTHEMUM
Bronze, gold, laven-
der, yellow, and white
Hope, Abundance

DAISY POMPON
White, yellow, laven-
der, purple, bronze,
and bicolors
Beauty

DELPHINIUM,
HYBRID
Blue, lavender, pur-
ple, pink, and white
Swift, Lighthearted

GARDENIA
White
*Grace, Refinement,
Secret Love*

GERBERA DAISY
Pink, orange, red,
white, yellow,
and bicolors
Innocence

GINGER
Pink and red
Strength

GLADIOLUS
White, pink, red, yel-
low, peach, purple,
and bicolors
Natural Grace

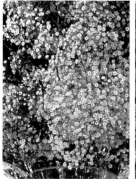
GYPSOPHILA,
MILLION STAR
White or pink

HEATHER
Rose, white, lavender

HELICONIA

HELICONIA,
HANGING

HELICONIA,
HONEYCOMB

HYDRANGEA
Blue, green, pink,
and white

HYPERICUM

KALANCHOE
PLANT,
POTTED YELLOW

LILY,
ENCHANTMENT
Orange

LILY, ORIENTAL
White and pink

LILY, STARGAZER
White and pink

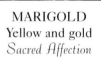
MARIGOLD
Yellow and gold
Sacred Affection

ORCHID,
CYMBIDIUM
Pink, white, green,
lavender, and yellow

ORCHID,
DENDROBIUM
Lavender, white,
pink, and bicolors

ORCHID, JAPHET
White and white
with a yellowish or
purple throat

ORCHID,
ONCIDIUM
Yellow
Love, Beauty

ORCHID,
PHALAENOPSIS
Lavender and white

PROTEA, BANKSIA

137

**PROTEA,
PIN CUSHION**
Pink, green, yellow,
orange, and red
Challenge of Desire

**PROTEA,
PINK FROST**

**QUEEN ANNE'S
LACE**
White
Self-reliance

ROSE
Ambiance

ROSE
Bluebird (Lavender),
Charlotte (Red),
Ravel (Pink)

ROSE
Champagne

ROSE
Confetti

ROSE
Leoniedas

ROSE
Pink Renata

ROSE
Sahara

ROSE
Versilia

ROSE
Virginia

ROSE
Vogue

ROSE
White Eskimo

SNAPDRAGON
White, pink, orange,
lavender, and yellow
Impetuous or Strength

STATICE
White, pink, and
purple

**STATICE,
GERMAN**
White

SUNFLOWER
Golden yellow
and brown
Power

TULIP
Red, pink, yellow,
orange, white,
and purple
Declare Your Love

VIKING POMPON
Yellow

WAX FLOWER
Pink and white

YARROW
Yellow and gold
Cure for Heartache

Foliage
CEDAR
Bright green
Strength

**CROTON
FOLIAGE**

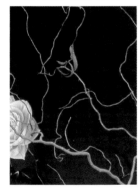

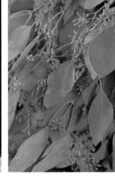

CURLY WILLOW
Greenish-tan

**DRACENA
FOLIAGE**

EQUISETUM

**EUCALYPTUS,
SEEDED**
Blue-green

**EUCALYPTUS,
SILVER DOLLAR**
Blue-green

**EUCALYPTUS,
SPIRAL**
Blue-green

FLAX
Domestic Symbol

**GUZMANIA
BETTINA
BROMELIAD
PLANT**

IVY
Deep green and varie-
gated varieties
*Wedded Love, Fidelity,
Friendship, Affection*

**IVY TOPIARY
PLANT, POTTED**

MING FERN
Bright green
Sincerity

**MONSTERA
FOLIAGE**

| MOSSY BRANCH | PLUMOSA FERN
Bright green | RAZOR BLADE
ACACIA
*Concealed Love or
Beauty in Retirement* | REINDEER MOSS | RUSCUS, ISRALIA
Dark green | RUSCUS, ITALIAN
Dark green |

  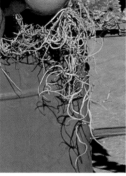   

| SALAL
(LEMON LEAF)
Dark green | SANSEVERIA
LEAVES | SNOWBERRY | SPANISH MOSS
*Maternal Love,
Charity* | STEEL GRASS
Submission | STRING OF
HEARTS |

| TI FOLIAGE | *Ornaments*
ARTICHOKE | BAMBOO
Peace | BREAD | BREADSTICK | BROCCOFLOWER
AND BRUSSEL
SPROUT |

CATTAIL
Peace, Prosperity

COCONUT
Abundance

DRIED GRAPEVINE
Charity, Mirth

DRIED POMEGRANATE
Elegance

DRIED WHEAT
Riches

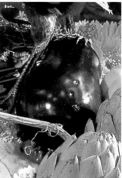

EGGPLANT

FLOWERING ARTICHOKE

GNARLY BRANCH

GOURD
Extent, Bulk

LEMON
Zest

LIME
Conjugal Love

LOTUS POD
Eloquence, Mystery, Truth

MINI GOURD

MINI PUMPKIN

NECTARINE

ORANGE

PEPPER

PINEAPPLE
Good Luck

PLUM
Fidelity

SEED BALL

SILK AFRICAN
VIOLET

SILK ONCIDIUM
ORCHID

SILK RED
CABBAGE

WHITE GRAPE
Charity, Mirth

The end

Metric Equivalency Chart

mm-millimetres cm-centimetres
inches to millimetres and centimetres

inches	mm	cm	inches	cm	inches	cm
⅛	3	0.3	9	22.9	30	76.2
¼	6	0.6	10	25.4	31	78.7
⅜	10	1.0	11	27.9	32	81.3
½	13	1.3	12	30.5	33	83.8
⅝	16	1.6	13	33.0	34	86.4
¾	19	1.9	14	35.6	35	88.9
⅞	22	2.2	15	38.1	36	91.4
1	25	2.5	16	40.6	37	94.0
1¼	32	3.2	17	43.2	38	96.5
1½	38	3.8	18	45.7	39	99.1
1¾	44	4.4	19	48.3	40	101.6
2	51	5.1	20	50.8	41	104.1
2½	64	6.4	21	53.3	42	106.7
3	76	7.6	22	55.9	43	109.2
3½	89	8.9	23	58.4	44	111.8
4	102	10.2	24	61.0	45	114.3
4½	114	11.4	25	63.5	46	116.8
5	127	12.7	26	66.0	47	119.4
6	152	15.2	27	68.6	48	121.9
7	178	17.8	28	71.1	49	124.5
8	203	20.3	29	73.7	50	127.0

yards to metres

yards	metres	yards	metres	yards	metres	yards	metres	yards	metres
⅛	0.11	2⅛	1.94	4⅛	3.77	6⅛	5.60	8⅛	7.43
¼	0.23	2¼	2.06	4¼	3.89	6¼	5.72	8¼	7.54
⅜	0.34	2⅜	2.17	4⅜	4.00	6⅜	5.83	8⅜	7.66
½	0.46	2½	2.29	4½	4.11	6½	5.94	8½	7.77
⅝	0.57	2⅝	2.40	4⅝	4.23	6⅝	6.06	8⅝	7.89
¾	0.69	2¾	2.51	4¾	4.34	6¾	6.17	8¾	8.00
⅞	0.80	2⅞	2.63	4⅞	4.46	6⅞	6.29	8⅞	8.12
1	0.91	3	2.74	5	4.57	7	6.40	9	8.23
1⅛	1.03	3⅛	2.86	5⅛	4.69	7⅛	6.52	9⅛	8.34
1¼	1.14	3¼	2.97	5¼	4.80	7¼	6.63	9¼	8.46
1⅜	1.26	3⅜	3.09	5⅜	4.91	7⅜	6.74	9⅜	8.57
1½	1.37	3½	3.20	5½	5.03	7½	6.86	9½	8.69
1⅝	1.49	3⅝	3.31	5⅝	5.14	7⅝	6.97	9⅝	8.80
1¾	1.60	3¾	3.43	5¾	5.26	7¾	7.09	9¾	8.92
1⅞	1.71	3⅞	3.54	5⅞	5.37	7⅞	7.20	9⅞	9.03
2	1.83	4	3.66	6	5.49	8	7.32	10	9.14

Index